"Bocchino transcends the clichés of her time for an artistic expression that feels truly visionary."

— Jonathan Goodman, Pratt Institute

SERENA BOCCHINO

THE ARTIST

SERENA BOCCHINO
THE ARTIST

Lisa A. Banner
Jonathan Goodman
Kathleen Goncharov

Edited by Lily Zhang

Special thanks to Basil Alkazzi for his generous support of this publication.

Abstracted Melodies: The Paintings and Techniques of Serena Bocchino © Lisa A. Banner

Foreword © Kathy Goncharov

Serena Bocchino: Jazz, Painterly Abstraction and the Tenacity of the New York School © Jonathan Goodman

Seeing: East Meets West © Lily Zhang

Photography
Chris DeLorenzo, Robert Foster, David Leonard, Jason Schuler, SGF Studios, and Zindman/Fremont

Designed by Lily Zhang

Thank you to Gayle Shimoun

All works by Serena Bocchino © Serena Bocchino

All rights reserved. No part of this publication may be reproduced or transmitted in any form or by any means, electronic or mechanical, including photocopy, recording or any other information storage and retrieval system, or otherwise without written permission from the publisher.

Library of Congress Control Number 2015934813
ISBN 978-0-9961443-0-8

140 pages, 121 illustrations, set in Calibri

Published by In His Perfect Time

Printed by CRW Graphics
Printed in USA

Cover Photo
Bocchino working in studio, Hoboken, NJ
Jason Schuler, 2013

Page 2
Over It, 2015
Enamel paint and mirrors on canvas
32 x 42 in.

Page 4
Artist in Observer Highway studio, Hoboken, NJ
David Leonard, 2002

CONTENTS

9   *Foreword*
Kathleen Goncharov

13   *Serena Bocchino: Jazz, Painterly Abstraction and the Tenacity of the New York School*
Jonathan Goodman

31   *Abstracted Melodies: The Paintings and Techniques of Serena Bocchino*
Lisa A. Banner

39   *Abstracted Melodies: The Paintings and Techniques of Serena Bocchino*
1990 to Present
Lisa A. Banner

65   **Publications**
1986 to 2003

71   *Seeing: East Meets West*
Lily Zhang

73   **Paintings and Installations**
2015 to 1987

125   **Drawings and Prints**
2015 to 1987

139   **Curricula Vitae**
Serena Bocchino

Cracked House Looking Up, 1988
Charcoal and graphite on rag paper
22.5 x 28.5 in.

FOREWORD

Kathleen Goncharov

Serena Bocchino's work first caught my eye at the Brodsky Center for Innovative Editions where she created a remarkable print with sensuous lines and luscious colors expertly combined and aptly titled *Simpatico*. I was familiar with her prints and works on paper, a medium in which she excels, but my first experience with her painting was at a visit to an impressive solo exhibition with the equally evocative title *Fever*.

"Fever", the song Peggy Lee made famous, celebrates the fire of love. I found that Serena had perfectly visualized the rhythms of the music and the sexy passion of the lyrics. She poured flaming red enamel paint over improvised graphite marks to create dramatic and sinuous lines that range from feather-thin to bold and dense. The subtle variations between these looping contrapuntal lines are complemented and punctuated with passages of gold leaf. These shimmering spots intensify the sizzle of the work and reflect the heat of its title and the words of the song.

The poetry embodied in this series of works is beautifully captured in a short film of the same title, "Fever". Bocchino's dynamic and energetic process is a perfect fit for the moving image; so this is only one of several films that document her unique painting methodology. Many have been screened on PBS and have won awards and even represented the United States at an International Film Festival at the Museum of Modern Art in New York.

Music is an important underpinning for Bocchino's work as it was for her artistic heroes, the Abstract Expressionists. For Pollock and New York School painters such as Lee Krasner, Willem de Kooning, and Norman Lewis, jazz was the key that unlocked the mind and tapped into the creative unconscious.

Serena Bocchino's musical interests are more eclectic than her predecessors and run the gamut from Leonard Bernstein to John Cage, as well as the great masters of jazz, John Coltrane and Miles Davis. She was exposed to music at an early age by her artist mother and even attended master classes at Julliard. Her exposure to all of the arts that New York City offers including dance, poetry and theater led Bocchino to conceive of art as an expression that goes beyond the limitations of medium. She thinks of her paintings as total works that encompass the performing as well as the visual arts, albeit in two dimension. She has described her painting as a kind of improvised opera that incorporates music, theatre and dance.

This need for artistic discovery through improvisation and introspection has not diminished since the time of Abstract Expressionism and Bocchino has embraced this quest with a singular fervor and talent. In today's market the art media pays the most attention to the clean lines of neo-Pop artists such as Jeff Koons and Damien Hirst, but the strain of art that Bocchino exemplifies is alive and well. Jean-Michel Basquiat's methods were improvisational; Louise Bourgeouis was deeply attuned to the unconscious; David Hammons regularly quotes jazz; and Sterling Ruby's abstract canvases are sprayed and splattered. Expressionism is still celebrated in Europe, especially in Germany where artists such as Anselm Kiefer and Georg Baselitz are revered.

Serena Bocchino joins a long list of artists throughout history who have looked to their predecessors for inspiration and a starting point from which to develop their own unique vision. Advances in all fields of human endeavor come from standing on the shoulders of giants and Serena Bocchino has chosen to learn from the Abstract Expressionists. She expertly appropriates techniques and ideas first developed in the 1950s and adapts them to her own needs in order to create personal and original work. It is often said that painting is dead, but like Mark Twain's death this is greatly exaggerated. Serena Bocchino is just one of a younger generation of artists who wholeheartedly embraces and celebrates this supposedly extinct medium.

BLUE Exhibition, 2007
Tria Gallery
New York, NY

SERENA BOCCHINO: JAZZ, PAINTERLY ABSTRACTION, AND THE TENACITY OF THE NEW YORK SCHOOL

Jonathan Goodman

Serena Bocchino, a New York artist to the utmost, creates powerful paintings rooted to the tradition of modern and contemporary painting. As someone who takes a strong interest in a historically aware, intellectual approach to art, she makes abstract paintings that reflect two quintessentially urban traditions: jazz and the New York School. Bocchino is a painter practicing in the still young century, and part of her challenge is to devise a bridge between the work of her artist predecessors and the current spirit of the time. It is true that both jazz and Abstract-Expressionist art have been sidelined a bit, in favor of a popular culture that despite its populism emphasizes other attributes, such as a greater conceptualism in art. But it also can be said that the improvisatory spirit in New York remains alive and well, even now, after a heyday that took place in the previous century; established women artists such as Joan Snyder and Louise Fishman continue to work ambitiously and effectively in the New York School style. Additionally, her free-wheeling abstract style bears the influence of artists like Matta, some of the Surrealist painters, Kandinsky, John Cage, even Matisse. Bocchino's strength as a painter is such that she matches the New York legacy she was given as an art student who received her master's degree from New York University. Her urban credentials from the 1980s are impressive—Bocchino worked as the assistant of Susan Rothenberg when the latter lived in New York, and has been friendly with a number of the outstanding artists of that generation.

Bocchino's upbringing was artistic; surrounded by books, she grew attached to reading at an early age. Her mother, very artistic herself, would make collages and assemblages from pages cut from books. Early on, Bocchino began studing the art of DaVinci and Michelangelo, as well as looking at and copying Old Master drawings and paintings. Given her mother's culture and creativity, Bocchino was introduced to classical opera and music. It is clear that she grew up in a very stimulating environment. In art, Bocchino developed an appreciation for master painters; in particular John Singer Sargent became a strong focus of Bocchino's study—she intensively reworked his brushwork and compositions. So early on she painted traditionally. However, despite this interest in realism, she was equally taken with abstraction. She loved Barnett Newman's *Stations of the Cross* at the National Gallery in Washington, D.C., as well as the works of Franz Kline and the sculptures and paintings of Giacometti. In college, Matta was an influence, in addition to the work of Arshile Gorky and Philip Guston, the color paintings of Mark Rothko, and the austere integrity of Clyfford Still. Matisse's color theory and the complex compositional treatments by Bonnard interested her. Mondrian's journey to total abstraction made a deep impression, as did Richard Diebenkorn's changing imagery. In fact, the color of the Bay Area painters showed her how to use bold, loud color—this was a big departure for Bocchino.

In all of Bocchino's series, the physicality of painting and an emphasis on a painting process is essential to her investigations as an artist. Her sequences of paintings are key to the way she works, with themes and ideas being repetitively explored in related groups of paintings. She is committed to treating abstraction as a high point in the art of her time—the brushstroke, in her hands a complete musical movement, is very important for her. As has been noted, Bocchino was an earnest student of art history. Earlier studies of the Renaissance masters, Goya, and Rembrandt, as well as later important figures such as the Pre-Raphaelists, Gainsborough, and John Singer Sargent (see illustration on page 18) prepared her for a commitment to painting. More recent artistic influences include Philip Guston, Alice Neel, Louise Nevelson, Lois Lane, and Susan Rothenberg—artists Bocchino would be highly familiar with as an active participant in the East Village movement.

Bocchino has had the good fortune to be in a center of art-making in the 1980s, a very auspicious time for painting in New York. The origins of the New York School are more than slightly magical, with Abstract Expressionism attaining a zenith in the 1940s and early '50s. Jazz at this moment was also at a high point. And the tradition goes on, as has been noted above. In America we still place a high value on being in the moment and return to examples of improvisation, which

Portrait, 1985
New York University Graduate Program

Kitchen of Violins (detail), 1988
PS1 Studio Residency
Oil on canvas
72 x 80 in.

Calling All Angels, 1989
Oil and graphite on canvas
20 x 36 in.
Private Collection

now have an established history but also offer an ongoing freedom to artists who want to press on in painterly abstraction. It is clear, relatively early on in Bocchino's career, that she has wanted to work with the gesture and also has made jazz both a medium and a metaphor for her art. This is not to say she has completely avoided figuration; her work as a student reflects a command of representational painting. And as it has often been said, we tend to trust a painter's abstraction more if we know that it has been preceded by a stint in realism. So Bocchino has not let completely go of her youthful ties to representational art; even now, in mid-career, she will include a bar staff with parts of actual songs in her paintings. The point to be made here is that a proficient artist's output is never entirely nonobjective or representational; passages in the same painting can suggest both. Additionally, one of the most important attributes of Bocchino's work is its use of color. A professor of hers in college, Voy Fangor, had a major impact on the artist's life; he was responsible for teaching Bocchino how to use color. According to the artist, "Voy made colors sing and taught us how to do that too!"

Bocchino received her undergraduate education at Fairleigh Dickinson University in New Jersey, where the artist Arie Galles taught her a good deal about composition and the application of paint in art. Later, at New York University, artists Robert Kaupelis, John Kacere, and Adelle Weber challenged Bocchino about what she painted and why she painted; they opened up to her the possibilities of the New York art world. At the time the East Village movement was in high swing, proving an inspiration to Bocchino, who immersed herself in its context and learned about art outside school. Her teachers encouraged her to see as much as possible, for New York was then (and still is) a world center for art of all periods. Music was also part of the adventure. Morris Golde, a patron of the arts, introduced Bocchino to the giants of the time, the avant-garde musical, dance, and literary intelligentsia: John Cage and Merce Cunningham; composers Leonard Bernstein and Ned Rorem; the poet and art critic John Ashbery and writer Maggie Paley. During this period, Bocchino attended master classes at Julliard, the ballet at Lincoln Center, concerts at the New York Philharmonic and contemporary dance by the Eric Hawkins Dance Company.

Portrait of Man, 1979
Oil on canvas
48 x 48 in.
Private Collection

After John Singer Sargent, 1980
Oil on canvas
36 x 34 in.
Private Collection

Bocchino feels that her breakthrough as an artist came relatively early, once she began painting at New York University. Taking as her ambition the creation of a Gesamtkunstwerk, her goal was to bring dance, music, and theater all together in a two-dimensional plane. The experience of all the arts were to inform her work; as she says, "Each painting was to be an opera." In 1987, Bocchino was awarded a residency at PS1, where she began to incorporate what she calls "the improvisational qualities and romantic notions" of jazz and the masters of jazz. Bocchino chose the saxophone as the symbol of musical passion, making that instrument a chief element in her paintings. Jazz does serve as a major metaphor and also central theme of her sensibility, but it should be remembered that the theme of jazz isn't the only focus of the various series Bocchino has produced. Another important aspect of her creativity has to do with performance, an understandable topic since Bocchino's art is itself a performed activity.

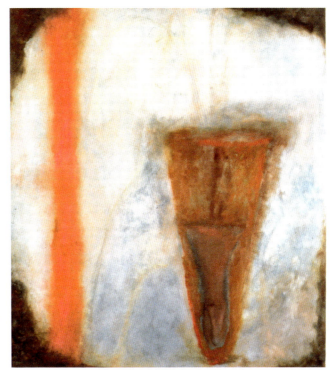

SideSax, 1988
PS1 Studio Residency
Oil on canvas
65 x 52 in.

Viewers of Bocchino's art find that more than three decades ago she was considerably fluent in treating her themes. An early painting, *SideSax*, (1988) shows a sax pointed straight ahead to the viewer, with a light-modeled background with a pink band. The image is abstract enough to take a bit of time for Bocchino's audience to fully comprehend, but it is in fact a musical instrument with the sky encompassing it—a nice joining of imagery. The sax of course is central to jazz; Bocchino's age group grew up on rock and roll, but, interestingly, she herself jumped backward a generation or two and grew attached to the earlier accomplishments of jazz music. The theme of improvisation, taken from music to serve as an equivalent for visual art, has provided Bocchino with a long-lasting content. At the same time, it is also important to emphasize her commitment to the art and poetry of the period. The intellectualism and spirituality of jazz is deeply important to her. So the dual purpose of music in her paintings gives her the motivation and the freedom to render as expansively as she can. Her love of music is possible to see in several short films made about Bocchino when she was a young artist. The footage emphasizes her handling of paint—in the films she paints on glass, echoing similar films of Picasso working, to help the viewer understand her process—and uses jazz as a wordless accompaniment to the art.

Inevitably, then, music and visual imagination are intertwined in Bocchino's art. Both serve as vehicles for each other. In a larger sense, the emphasis on an improvised creativity is thoroughly American; we still value freedom in art as a primary attribute of its integrity. Nonetheless, the question must be asked: Is such an understanding of painting vigorous at this point in time? New York's contemporary cultural life has become saturated with striving artists and art styles; no particular method of working exists. The age of pluralism, begun in New York in the 1970s, continues to this day. In this sense, Bocchino has every right to push forward with a historically considered style of painting. Her art makes use of the past, and we know that, now, Abstract Expressionism persists in a time when many kinds of art vie for attention. But Bocchino's motivation and circumstances are valid in the sense that they remain part of the current mix.

So it is fair to assert that Bocchino has every right to proceed as she knows best. Her paintings take the position that their historical contextualization strengthens their appeal; additionally, they are able to move us as art precisely because they can be identified within a particular convention. Thus, their placement in time is a bit flexible. Like all good art, they come from an established place but proceed toward and into a new language, one that is Bocchino's own. No artist can go on without coming from a specific position; but it is equally evident that painters must strive to develop their own voice, one appropriate for the new circumstances every generation must face. In Bocchino's case, we see that her work embodies a style both historical and present-tense; in many ways, she builds a continuum with the spirit of our time.

The new, young artists will look to Bocchino and her generation just as she and they look to their predecessors, in a language that quotes a style begun in the middle of the 20th century. With gestural abstraction being what it is, and having the history that it does, the effort of representing the new grows more difficult as time goes on. Perhaps this is why Bocchino turns to another genre of art as the theme of her work. In jazz, musicians now have their own legacy to transform, so their situation is much like that of artists. Bocchino shows us how she shares the challenge of artistic renewal with other abstract painters, who emphasize space and color and whose formalism can emphasize intellect over feeling—a stance Bocchino doesn't share. In the realm of painting, later on in Bocchino's career women artists such as Jennifer Bartlett, Joan Mitchell, Helen Frankenthaler, Pat Steir, Susan Rothenberg, and Elizabeth Murray provided examples of heroism for a young artist in love with the productions of the New York School.

Actually, Bocchino has a bit of an advantage as a painter; her possibilities are both representational and abstract. This is where painting excels in current terms: in the presentation of nonobjective and figurative imagery at the same time. It is true that much of what Bocchino does seems, on first glance, pretty thoroughly nonobjective; yet she does in fact bring into play an imagery that references music with recognizable objects like staffs and notes, so that she balances her abstract gestures with actual things. Like so many accomplished painters today, she stands on a middle ground—she is in between ways of seeing. But it is equilibrium fraught with a highly developed sense of self-awareness, which results from the distinct awareness of an artistic generation that must work in the shadow of giants. This is not Bocchino's fault, but it is the condition she must master; indeed, it is the situation we face in all the arts—music, poetry, theater, and dance. Time alone will reveal just how successfully the lessons of modernism have been revised. It is clear that Bocchino's work adds compellingly to the discussion.

Working in series, Bocchino creates a musical effect by creating related versions of imageries. Her *Fever* sequence incorporates graphite and poured enamel paint in the manner of Jackson Pollock. Inevitably, it also relates to jazz, bringing out with slightly raised imagery (from a greater paint density), a dimension in time. As she says in a quotation accompanying

99° Hold Me Tight (Fever Series), 2012
Enamel and gold leaf on canvas
42 x 52 in.
Private Collection

the series: "I am interested in a type of controlled spontaneity." This is key to her paintings, whose red swirls and dips, in some cases embellished with metal leaf, belong to the grand tradition of the New York School.

In *99° Hold Me Tight* (2012)—the title is a phrase from the song, "Fever"—Bocchino achieves an all-out effect more or less baroque in its visual enthusiasm. Red paint delineates a roughly circular motion, with gold leaf highlights filling gaps made by the enamel. Underneath, we see a pencil drawing on a roughly sketched grid, which is punctuated by a small, tight imagery of scribbles. The elegant circular swirls of the poured red paint contrast with the hand-drawn graphite imagery, which is rough and even messy. But the pattern also can connect with the general metaphor of jazz, in which tight flurries of notes spelling out a melody are quickly overwhelmed by an inspired succession of freely atonal music.

Music may well be the most universally received and appreciated contemporary genre, causing the distinction between high and low culture to disappear. But today the practice of fine art has of course become remarkably popular. At this point in time, we can see that it speaks to a new cohort of young artists intent upon esthetic and spiritual exploration. But we should remember that the long process of finding a voice remains the primary, if not the only, means of development (one of the problems of art today is that we are asking very young people to exhibit work that may not in fact be ready for the public). In Bocchino's situation, the support of music gives her a greater freedom and imaginative space to look into; in fact, it is central to her findings as a painter. Her music is our text, delivered to her audience in the guise of paint. We find her synesthesia to be of real interest; categories of esthetic assertion merge, hopefully offsetting the fragmented nature of culture now.

Bocchino's finely imagined world of music is inherently abstract, yet it is predicated on something that can be seen or envisioned. This places her art in the realm of that which can be rendered, with visual nods to actual objects in the world. The crimson spirals in *99° Hold Me Tight* inform the viewer of the delight of a song taken out of one context and incorporated into another. It is seeing quite literally in a different key. The other paintings in the sequence show us how Bocchino continues to refine her efforts in quoting a music which may originate in an earlier time, but which serves to educate her current audience about a certain inspired, even carefree attitude toward culture. Given today's overly professionalized, often careerist bent in the fine arts world, doing so amounts to a revelation to her viewers. By maintaining an open contact with the past, Bocchino makes it clear that we operate as artists in a continuum, a long line of practice that cannot be erased.

Today (detail), 2014
Enamel and gold leaf on mirror

This affords us a view of the past that is linked to a vision of the present and future.

The spacing and movement in another group of works by Bocchino, which she calls the *White Series*, show that the artist is fluent in her particular class of art. In these paintings and drawings, we watch her revert to the raw feeling of early Abstract Expressionism. She doesn't lose sight of her connection to music; one of the strongest works in the sequence is deftly named *Miles Blinks Again* (2002), a bold, billowing image of a gyre painted in black that refers to Miles Davis, the great jazz trumpeter. The picture begins with a narrow spiral at its

Miles Blinks Again, 2002
Enamel paint on canvas
42 x 51 in.

top, but then bulges out in the middle, growing narrow again at the bottom of the composition. Its series of controlled curves emulates the curling flight of notes we might hear in one of Davis' themes. The picture, nearly primal as well as very sophisticated, presents us with a fine space that visually embodies the joy of music. Really, her culture is American culture, which identifies with the transcendental moment. If her work were anything less than a comprehensive moment, the paintings would feel imitative. But her response maintains an integrity seen again and again in the found metaphor of music in her art.

Indeed, metaphor, a means of transforming imagination, is central to Bocchino's art. Unlike the symbol, which reifies the mind's action, a metaphor changes it to something else. If we look at another painting in the *White Series*, we can see how the artist's reliance on a deliberately limited palette actually frees her from the burden of excessive choice. Moreover, her use of music as a metaphor liberates her painting from the confines of its particular genre. We can see this take place in *Television* (2002) a spirited, spare work that repeats open rectangles on top of squares mostly filled in with light brown. An ode to the idiot's box, *Television* (2002) also sees the screen as an opportunity for form, with the black rectangles being outlined in tendrils of line. Such an alteration is both meaningful and funny and a little unusual for Bocchino, whose use of quotidian material tends to start higher up on the cultural ladder. Nonetheless, she has made use of a primal American artifact. It relates to her effective use of popular culture, beginning with jazz strains and culminating with something as banal as television, whose history dates back to the 1940s, when the Abstract Expressionists were at their height.

Bocchino's penchant for the demotic is a precedent for today's democratized culture. But it refers to a popular art that took place during what was likely a less polarized, more benevolent time. In today's art, we reflect, sometimes to the point of violence, not only current ideas but also what happened and, hopefully, what will come to be. The music of Bocchino's mentors was not so very historically minded, emphasizing instead a first-time, original presentation of musical ideas. Still, nothing in art now takes place in a historical void, so the creativity animating jazz, at its high point in the middle of the last century, had its beginnings in what preceded it. It becomes clear that Bocchino needs to quote her legacy; this enables her to move toward the new. As a result, Bocchino's painting *Television* (2002) opens our eyes to the visual possibilities of what many of us would liken to a vapid image; however, she changes the object to something far more lyrical.

It is true that Bocchino's visual effects can be described not only as musical but also as poetic. The *Twirl Series* is particularly enhanced by its poetic impressions; although the artist does not make mention of poetry, her paintings reveal a connection in the imaginative energy of the imagery, which salutes the gung-ho spirit of American creativity. When we say a picture is "poetic," we acknowledge the primacy of the imagination in its impact, just as we do something similar when we call an artwork "musical." Poetry's ability to call out thought, emotion, and form in words enables us to consider a verbally crafted expressiveness, but the genre can extend to other modes of expression as well. Music is the first choice of Bocchino in structuring much of her art, although it is fair to say that both realms, music and poetry, are suggested in her paintings.

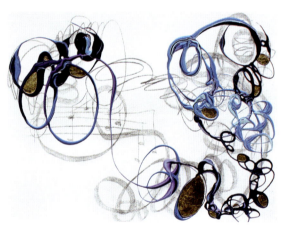

Star Dance Lead (Twirl Series), 2014
Enamel and gold leaf on canvas
38 x 48 in.

In *Star Dance Lead* (2014) Bocchino again employs enamel paint, applied gold leaf, and graphite, which establish a finely tuned perception of sound's spirited travel in the world. In the painter's hand, the blue-colored twirls and graphite drawing marks underneath demonstrate their capacity for coherent results; Bocchino has even included a musical staff and notes to demonstrate her affinity for harmony. But the effect of the painting is also lyrical; it depends on sensitivity to feeling that is close to poetry. Its youthful buoyancy refers to the emotion that all is going well, as happens a lot in the poetry of Frank O'Hara, an enthusiasm of Bocchino's when she was young.

There are times when one kind of art will supplant the achievements of another—for example, the achievements of music will be more relevant and far-reaching than literature or art. Yet, in Bocchino's paintings, she achieves a kind of weightlessness that springs from the equal use of two genres: music and art. The poetry I see in *Star Dance Lead* intensifies its ramifications; here the sum of the painting is greater than the discrete presentation of its parts. *Star Dance Lead* is representative of the general call-and-reply of Bocchino's creativity, in which the musical, the lyric, and the abstract are intertwined and vie equally for the viewer's attention. This kind of work is currently an international phenomenon: Bocchino can no longer assume that the tradition she interprets is evident to Americans alone, especially in New York. Now people for whom English is a second language make up a large part of her audience, and this results in a different engagement with the artist, one in which the response to her paintings is broadened and made more sophisticated.

It is interesting to speculate on Bocchino's accomplishments in light of the change in cultural background of her viewers. What will the future bring? Clearly, the Abstract Expressionist moment has been duplicated in other nations—we have only to think of Pierre Soulages, still living, in France; or Hans Hartung in Germany. But somehow America owns that point in cultural advancement; we continue within the confines of our heritage even as we persist in making it broader, more inclusive. And this is essentially the larger point of Bocchino's achievement: that is, the New York School endures, no matter the warning of critics who see an end of the long American century. One of the most intriguing—and compelling—aspects of New York culture now is the extent to which it has been made different by an esthetic globalism. But that has also been true from the start; both Willem de Kooning and Arshile Gorky, along with Pollock—the first members of the Abstract Expressionist movement—were foreigners.

Soul Shower II, 2000; Enamel and oil on canvas; 19 x 24 in. (left side)
Yesterday (White on White Series), 2014; Enamel and gold leaf on mirror and prepared canvas; 42 x 52 in. (center left)
Today (White on White Series), 2014; Enamel and gold leaf on mirror and prepared canvas; 42 x 52 in. (center right)

Bocchino, who has years of creativity remaining open to her, is poised to build an art advancing the genre. One hesitates to say that her art will "progress," as her art both circles around the past, but Bocchino is a good artist, and she moves forward in a contemporary use of imagery. Her idiom may be understood as attaining certain timelessness, in the sense that she reiterates a basic truth: the need to be anchored in time in order to push culture forward. Bocchino, like many of us in America, comes from immigrant forefathers—just as many young New York artists do. So her process, while based on a longer ancestral stay, mimics the way New York is now being enriched by art from many different geographies. Music remains highly popular today; it almost effortlessly internalizes international influences. So the poetry of Bocchino's visual choices is essentially correct; it reflects a reality more cultured, in a literal and a metaphorical sense, than what we might expect. It is fortunate that music can be visually imagined. This means that the artist can hold on to a double path of abstract expression and figurative rendering. This makes her paintings richer and more complex. She transcends the clichés of her time for an artistic expression that feels truly visionary.

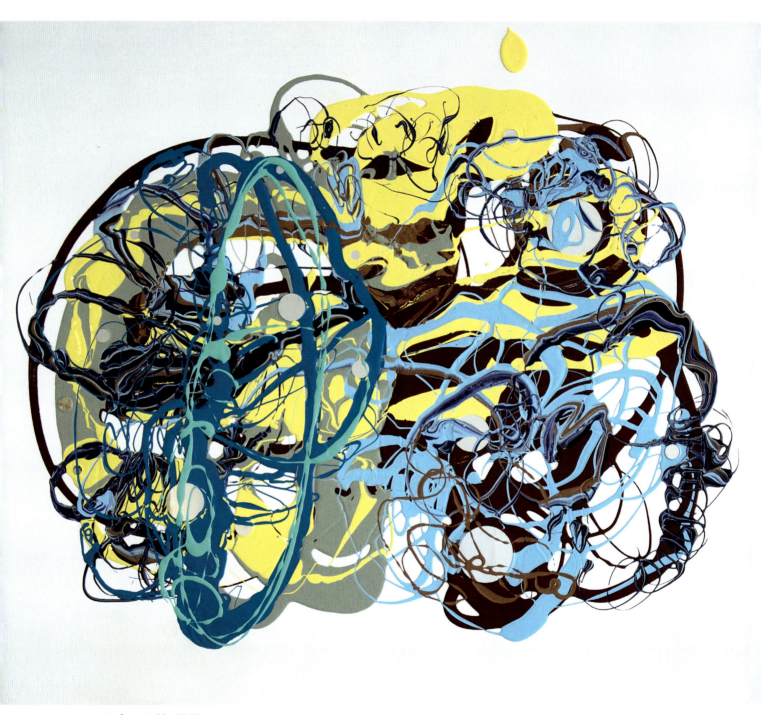

Unforgettable, 2015
Enamel on canvas
36 x 42 in.

ABSTRACTED MELODIES: THE PAINTINGS AND TECHNIQUES OF SERENA BOCCHINO

Lisa A. Banner

Music suffuses the large sunlit studio where Serena Bocchino paints. A lifelong influence upon her canvases, strains of classical and jazz music are as necessary as light and color for the paintings, drawings, and sculptures she creates. Often choosing to work in series, making paintings that involve a focused study of a single aspect of music or sound, and interpreting the sound through mark-making and color, Bocchino varies from small to large size canvases, at times augmenting them with canvas strips, fragments of mirror and other adhesions, in order to provide a transparent, interrupted, or reflective surface on which to begin painting. Gestural and purposeful drawings from the 1990s, stark charcoal swirls, offer a bold foil to the vibrant colors of her recent paintings. Yet each period of time shows a distinctive and holistic approach defined by choices of material and subject matter to achieve a cohesive body of work that shows a strong and determined forward progress. Subtly inflected with rhythmic movement, lyrical at times, and seductive at others, Bocchino's work is underscored by the constant presence of musical language—that language influences her shape, the color and movement in her painting. Under the paint, she often begins by drawing gestures that embody sound with a vigorous and clearsighted energy applied to the surface. In medium and in spirit, her work is motivated and directed by music.

Bocchino's career has been shaped by extraordinary relationships and serendipity. While in graduate school, she was chosen as a studio assistant to Susan Rothenberg, and in 1986, was invited to show with Rothenberg, Jenny Holzer, April Gornik and Eric Fischl. While she held a residency at PS1, she met several people who would later be influential for her career in the early 1990s. The Vice Prime Minister of Italy, Honorable Gianni De Michelis, saw Bocchino's work during an open studio visit, and as a result she was invited to show her work in Rome. Bocchino had her first international solo show at Studio Bocchi in Rome at his invitation in 1990. Although these are only a few of many fortuitous events and meetings she has had, they reflect the spontaneous and warm

Serena Bocchino

Catalogue
Studio Bocchi
Rome, Italy

Two Drums, 1986
Oil on canvas
46 x 42 in.

Susan Rothenberg, *Cabin Fever*, 1976
Acrylic and tempera on canvas
67 x 84-1/8 in.
Collection: Modern Art Museum of Fort Worth
© 2015 Susan Rothenberg/Artists Rights
Society (ARS), New York

nature that Serena Bocchino brings to her work, and how it is positively received by a variety of patrons. Solo shows thereafter have repeatedly caught the attention of critics from media as diverse as *The New Yorker*, *The New York Times*, *San Francisco Chronicle*, *ArtNews*, and *Art in America*.

Moving away from figurative work that she explored early on, and further developed in graduate school, Bocchino utilizes a number of media, frequently involving drawing practice. Yet she draws with poured paint, and gestural movement. Graphite and oil paint used together, recently on vellum paper, or a smooth support like mirror panel, provide other fresh surfaces with which she explores the movement of line over blank surfaces. Examples of her graphic works from the 1980s through the present demonstrate her commitment to experimenting with new media, one of the important features of her vibrant practice.

Layers of thoughtful preparation and accumulations of visual references mold the nuanced body of her paintings, and inflect the personal language of Serena Bocchino. The apparent influence of important painters like Helen Frankenthaler and Susan Rothenberg on her earliest paintings, and other more subtle influences connect Bocchino to a longer American and European tradition of abstraction and gestural painting. Lyrical and less apparent influences of Paul Klee, Joan Miró, Zao Wou-ki, Fernando Zóbel de Ayala, and even Franz Kline, have not been fully explored in analysis of Bocchino's work from the 1980s until now.

Departing from figurative classical training in painting, Bocchino began working on paint surfaces, altering perception of the forms that would later lead her to a more abstract style. Tangible and direct influences from Rothenberg's work manifest in the gauzy or filmy surfaces of paintings like *Two Drums*, from 1986. A pair of drums occupies the middle ground of the painting, silent and still reminders of sounds in the studio that might have led her to drift from the earlier concreteness of form. Disparity in the size of the two drums catches the viewer's attention. The taller of the two African drums has a narrow base and wider throat, with loops of leather for handholds around the sides. The smaller drum, shapely and slightly green, glows as if vibration from recent play still emanates from its surface. A dynamically muted painting, *Two Drums* showcases Bocchino's relationship to a symbolic object, the drum, that recalls the importance of the percussive line underneath a melody, like a heartbeat under the weight of days. Similar to Rothenberg's iconic horses, Bocchino's paintings of musical instruments like this one encourage the viewer to connect the symbol to what is not present, strains of music that inspired her work. Earthy colors chosen for their subtle relationships, are daubed onto the surface in short viscous strokes. Suggesting

Church of the Immaculate Conception
414 East 14th Street
New York, NY

9 Bells, 1986
Oil on canvas
72 x 72 in.
Private Collection

an energetic strain of jazz, the two drums lead the viewer to revel in the surface of the painting. A ground layer, thin yet rich in color, provides all the setting that is needed for objects at the heart of the composition. Still decidedly figurative at this moment, Bocchino directly explored the importance of sound and color in her work; but it is in this painting that she takes a decisive step toward the later more abstracted melodies in painting.

Also from this critical year, *9 Bells* was completed in the artist's studio at 405 East 13th Street. Bocchino sublet studio space from artist Fred Wilson; the environment of the Lower East Side during those years was rich with possibility. The building was owned by Larry Rivers, and gathered a number of artists together in close proximity, fertile ground for the exchange of ideas. Bocchino recalls the intimate community, the frequency of studio visits, and even walking with large paintings down several city blocks to exhibit them.

The composition of *9 Bells* evokes the movement that accompanies sound. The church nearby (Immaculate Conception Parish in New York City), where bells ring at 9 am or 9 pm, provided the sound that the painter interpreted, literally, with nine bells marking the hour. Three bells in the center of the upper register are flanked by moving strings of other bells that seem to swing into the space below.

As Bocchino continued working for Rothenberg, the influence on her technique was expressed in paintings like *Soul Sax*, where physical form of the instrument is symbolic of the artist's relationship to sounds emanating from it. Ghostly aspects of the instrument's mouthpiece, prominent color and shape of the throat of the sax suggest forward movement of sound from inside the instrument. A river of magenta paint separates mid-ground from foreground, placing the viewer in front of a snowy swath at bottom, isolated from warmth emanating from the instrument. Nuanced gray background fascinates as the sax emerges from a light-infused surrounding. A ball of white at the left edge of the canvas anticipates Bocchino's series of burst paintings that follow in the next decade, where she applied abstraction to the expression of light and substance.

Drawings from the late 1980s and early 1990s, created while Bocchino held a residency at PS1, are among the most expressive works from this period. Reserved paper creates emptiness at the composition center and resounds to the gestural force of black smears and strokes. In the *Eurekasax* drawing, charcoal and graphite define forms, then blur and dissolve. Sharp forms in black shape the white space at the center, and varied strokes of charcoal are smeared and rubbed across the paper. The composition is a moving poem about the instrument.

Soul Sax, 1987
Oil on canvas
60 x 40 in.

EurekaSax, 1988
Charcoal and graphite on paper
30 x 22 in.

EurekaSax, 1988
Oil on canvas
52 x 48 in.
Private Collection

ABSTRACTED MELODIES: THE PAINTINGS AND TECHNIQUES OF SERENA BOCCHINO
1990 to Present

Stand, 1992
Oil and collage on canvas
18 x 18 in.

Franz Kline, *Painting No. 2*, 1954
Oil on canvas
80 in. x 107 in.
Collection: Museum of Modern Art, New York
© 2015 The Franz Kline Estate/Artists Rights Society (ARS), New York

Through the 1990s and into the early 2000s, her pace began to quicken and Bocchino worked in series, exploring single themes in variation, concentrating effort on varying support size, strength of line, or media on different surfaces.

Paintings from the early 1990s investigated what canvas would hold, literally, as Bocchino added collage elements to the surfaces. *Stand*, from 1992, originally begun on the wall, recalls Franz Kline (1910-1962). Bocchino used a canvas strip that was created independently with paint and graphite in order to interrupt and add a fragmentary element to the surface of this canvas. *Stand* demonstrates her forceful yet nuanced process, where the artist used a silkscreening squeegee to spread paint, creating unique marks by sweeping and pushing paint against canvas. After initial marks were laid down, she elaborated the composition with brush strokes, and added the unconventional tool of wires dipped in paint and laid against canvas. She also employed wires inserted into a tube of paint, withdrawn, loaded with paint and placed against canvas for variety of effect, deliberately achieving thick and thin lines.

Franz Kline's black and white abstractions also explore positive and negative space created by gestural strokes in thick black oil paint on imposing white canvases, like *Chief* (Museum of Modern Art, New York), dating from 1950, or *Painting Number 2*, from 1954 (Museum of Modern Art, New York). But in small scale works, for example *Untitled II*, from circa 1952, he used ink and oil on telephone book pages, making gestures with simple, expressive strokes, in dense black ink and oil; at times he collaged several pieces of paper onto a stronger support.

These works are both calligraphic and meditative, recalling traditional Chinese calligraphy, where the gesture becomes a statement and is connected to profound spiritual exercises. Bocchino's

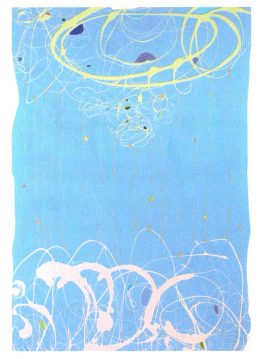

Jazz Fountain Falls (Catch Series), 2006
Enamel and oil on canvas
80 x 60 in.

Zao Wou-Ki (1921-2013), *The Night is Stirring*, 1956
Oil on linen 76-1/5 x 51 in.
Collection: The Art Institute of Chicago
© 2015 Artists Rights Society (ARS),
New York/ProLitteris, Zurich

charcoal and graphite drawing *EurekaSax*, although several years earlier, anticipates the sophistication of gestural composition she achieves in *Stand*, black and white oil on canvas; although quite small, *Stand* incorporates a gestural calligraphic element.

Abstract drawings and paintings of Zao Wou-ki (1921-2013) are invoked in these and later works by Bocchino, where an authoritative directional gesture forms the heart of the composition. Zao's painting from 1956, *The Night is Stirring* (Art Institute of Chicago), is a powerful address to unspoken emotions and thoughts. Abstraction, his universal language, is married with poetic titles to evoke our response. These find echoes in Bocchino's paintings, like *Jazz Fountain Falls*, or *Untitled Fountain*, 2006 from the *Catch Series*, in oil and graphite on vellum. The energetic linearity of Bocchino's composition is similar to the rising pillar of night expressed with dark blues and reds in Zao's composition. The explosive nature of Bocchino's line, blue dashes against a netted, loosely squared background in *Untitled Fountain*, creates a dynamic composition against the grid restraint, like the poetic dark force in Zao's *Night is Stirring* rises against plain canvas.

Bocchino combines the language of figures and abstraction, reminding us of playful drawings by Paul Klee, where that dialogue acquires a new vocabulary. Klee's *Abstract Trio*, a

Untitled Fountain, 2006
Oil and graphite on vellum
11 x 14 in.

Untitled Squeegee Drawing, 1993
Oil and graphite on rag paper
22 x 30 in.

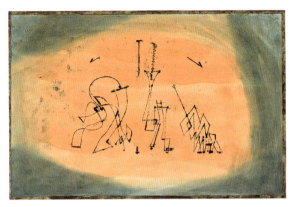

Paul Klee (German, 1879–1940), *Abstract Trio*, 1923
Watercolor and transferred printing ink on paper, bordered with gouache and ink
12-1/2 x 19-3/4 in.
The Berggruen Klee Collection, 1984 (1984.315.36)

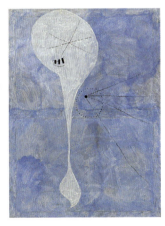

Juan Miró
Personage, 1925
Oil and egg tempera on canvas
51-1/4 x 37-7/8 in.
Solomon R. Guggenheim Museum, New York
Estate of Karl Nierendorf, by purchase
© 2015 Successió/ Artists Rights Society (ARS), New York/ ADAGP, Paris 2015

watercolor and transferred ink work on paper, presents three primary figures, reminiscent of musical instruments, in the center of a blue green swirl. The forms create a harmony of implied sound, held at the center, and enveloped within the green embrace of a gouache and watercolor band. Bocchino's *Jazz Fountain Falls*, or her *Untitled BL002*, oil paint and graphite on vellum paper, similarly involve the rhythm of three abstracted segments, where suffused color holds the composition.

Jazz Fountain Falls, a large abstraction from 2006, forces the viewer's eye to travel, following effusions of white tangles at the top of the canvas. Slipping down the streamers of white to the bottom edge of the canvas, the eye rests and flows with the paint. Like vertical contrails from an airplane, the loose lines fall away from the tangle, into three columns, pulled and resolved as they slip down the surface of the blue canvas, becoming restful and elongating, stretching through the blue.

It might be related to Miró's Blue paintings, I, II, and III a triptych from 1961, which involve a saturated blue canvas and precisely arranged symbols, or Miró's *Personage* of 1925 (Guggenheim, New York), an oil and egg tempera painting, that focuses on the intensity and softness of a gauzy blue, and finds a figural form at its heart. Bocchino's *Jazz Fountain Falls*, full of energetic and dangling lines as opposed to Miró's quiet, extruded form, also explores the heart of blue pigment and surrounds form with color.

Here, from 1999, painted with enamel and oil is a small work that achieves a balanced exploration of the surface with the delicate lines and filled forms that recall Paul Klee's use of color

Untitled BL002 (Catch Series), 2006
Oil and graphite on vellum paper
19 x 29 in.

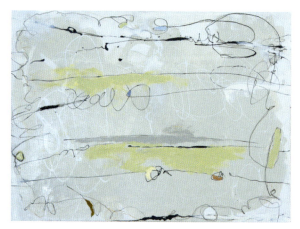

Here (White Series), 1999
Oil, enamel and graphite on canvas
30 x 40 in.

and line on a neutral background. Patterning and layering, at the heart of Bocchino's painting practice, are artfully resolved with the daubs of spring green and crocus purple, white, blue and orange dots, and smears that appear in intervals, caught up by the threads of line. Horizon lines, almost making a landscape appear over the green central band of color, create an abstracted landscape in the heart of the painting, with a grey cloud rising above a defined graphite line.

In the late 1990s, Bocchino allowed music itself to begin to permeate the articulation of her paintings, combining drawing media like graphite, and oil paint together on canvases, and then beginning to let her hand wander over the surface, pouring and dripping, and letting the paint itself begin to work on the canvas, or vellum support, and find its own way.

In works like *Untitled* of 1998, horizontal bands of dark green oil paint are laid with the brush, and then allowed to trickle into the reserved white of her vellum support. Red splotches interfere with yellow, becoming a smear of orange, and at times remaining whole and contained.

Untitled, 1998
Oil and graphite on vellum
24 x 36 in.

Horizontal painting becomes a narrative of sounds filtering through Bocchino's mind, playing in the studio, like stride piano by Willie "the Lion" Smith, or flamboyant, exhilarating jazz sung by Bessie Smith.

While not direct conscious influences or visual precedents, Kline's and Zao's works convey similar concerns that Bocchino explores in a variety of media. *Tango Hip* from 1997, is an exploration of pure motion. The lyrical abstraction of painters like Helen

Frankenthaler, who soaked canvases with paint while they lay on the floor, and allowed paint to move and stain swaths of color onto her canvas, is clearly a major influence on Bocchino. Frankenthaler's epic 1952 *Mountains and Sea*, Collection: Helen Frankenthaler Foundation (on extended loan to the National Gallery of Art, Washington, D.C.), was painted with a fresh palette similar to Bocchino's 1997 *Tango Hip*. Green lines loop over pinks and pale lavenders, with blue and darting orange highlights, evoke a springtime dance. Frankenthaler's painting asserts a landscape vision, while Bocchino's depicts a dance in space; both are saturated with pure color in movement. Pouring paint onto the canvas is how Serena Bocchino activates a lyrical movement over the surface, where the hand does not touch the stroke of color laid down. Allowing musical rhythm to guide her hand, Bocchino adds poured and spilt lines in deliberate and expressive motions, as she says, "drawing with poured paint".

Echoes for Ella, 1998
Oil and graphite on canvas
38 x 48 in
Private Collection.

Tango Hip of 1997, and *Echoes for Ella* of 1998, both oil and graphite on canvas, were shown widely in a show organized by Ben Shahn Galleries in 1998. Both recall Ella Fitzgerald's version of "Hernando's Hideaway," a tango-rhythm torch song about a speakeasy, the strike of a match, and the secluded place of faceless seduction. Swirling green strokes over the surface recall movements of a tango dancer, oblique green ovals tracing movements through space. Small glittering gold and orange spots recall cigarettes glowing in blue darkness. Castanets and percussion are visible in round repeated forms and softer colors.

Helen Frankenthaler
Mountains and Sea, 1952
Oil and charcoal on canvas
86-5/8 x 117-1/4 in.
Collection: Helen Frankenthaler Foundation (on extended loan to the National Gallery of Art, Washington, D.C.)
© 2015 The Helen Frankenthaler Foundation, Inc./Artists Rights Society (ARS), New York

Tango Hip, 1997
Oil and graphite on canvas
40 x 46 in.
Private Collection

Ella's constant mix of blues, jazz and scat, featured voice as percussive instrument, melody and highlight. *Echoes for Ella* has a playful surface, where Bocchino translates a visual record of throaty sensual notes, gestural vocals. Ella's classics "Cry Me a River," "Night and Day," and with Louis Armstrong, "Summertime," feature rich mellow voice, loaded warm notes, moving easily from over the scales. In *Echoes for Ella*, Boccchino takes a neutral ground, a beige cement colored paint smoothed over the canvas center, evoking Ella's voice, using graphite to link several elements of sound colors: red, gold, grey and lavender. The fluid energy expressed in sound is felt in the music, with colors in motion, connecting Bocchino's painting to its source.

The work anticipates Bocchino's *Fever Series* from 2012, with direct reference to a song written by Eddie Cooley and Otis Blackwell, made famous by Little Willie John and covered by Peggy Lee. Taking titles from lyrics, Bocchino's *Fever Series* features red smears of enamel paint, varying

Covered (Fever Series), 2012
Enamel, gold leaf and graphite on canvas
24 x 24 in.

103° When You Call My Name (Fever Series), 2013
Enamel, gold leaf and graphite on canvas
68 x 72 in.

Everybody's Got the Fever (Fever Series), 2013
Enamel paint, gold leaf and graphite on canvas
50 x 36 in.

from viscous lacquered Chinese red to persimmon orange. Highlights in gold and silver leaf are carefully hand-rubbed in glittering flat forms laid into the embrace of the red lines.

"Fever" employs sultry and evocative vocals, snapping fingers, and simple bass accompaniment to stir up trouble. Bocchino plays with this metaphor in paintings like *Covered Fever*, and *103° Fever When You Call My Name* where she poured ribbons of red enamel paint like moving fabric over the surface of the canvas. In *Everybody's Got the Fever*, graphite musical notes intrude, and describe her inspiration.

Bocchino cites influences in addition to the pervasive suave effect of music. Paintings by Mark Rothko, Clyfford Still, and Joan Mitchell are foremost. Yet Helen Frankenthaler's inspiration on Bocchino's process is also unmistakable, a subconscious infiltration. The most obvious influence on the early paintings, Rothenberg, was achieved through direct involvement in her studio where Bocchino was employed during graduate school. Rothenberg's influence is evident in the gauzy surfaces of Bocchino's early paintings, where a sort of haze blurs lines and edges, softening and dissipating the forms. Later works veer into a new realm, allowing paint to become deeply, thickly viscous on the surfaces, and creating linear designs over layers of drawing, and paint preparation. An inescapable comparison to the paintings of Cy Twombly, especially when looking at Bocchino's more recent works, suggests that her paintings contain the same sort of contemplative, rhythmic movement and sweeping gesture that mesmerizes the surface of his painted works. Bocchino's intuitive large gestures of linear swirls over large swaths of color and her delicate tracery over complex layers, entwine the viewer in a visual landscape of depth and smoothness.

Among the most important of Bocchino's production over the last twenty years, a few of the works from 1992 stand out, where her developing visual language began to find a toothy expression in black and white. *Stand*, from 1992, is a symphony of line and blotchy thick black against a raw canvas. Echoes of Paul Klee, Franz Kline, and Cy Twombly dominate the painting, which is among the finest of a series of small works Bocchino made around this time. Yet when taken in the whole of her oeuvre, the sort of impulse of the dark series, with black strokes, held against the white of the canvas, and then a later white on white series, also recalls the wispy and attenuated lines of the mid-century painter, Fernando Zóbel de Ayala. Paintings and sketches by Zóbel often reveal a dreamy, contained abstraction in the center of a canvas or a sheet of paper. *Stand's* smeared layers of black, with tonal variation, describe the same impulses expressed in *The Dream of the Damsel* (Harvard Art Museum, Cambridge). *Untitled for Missing Mingus*, from 2000, oil paint and graphite on vellum, explores the same tonal variations that we see in Zóbel's *Dream*. Think of Charles Mingus' "Moanin'" playing in that sunlit studio where Bocchino paints, bright high brass notes and the interactive energy of sax and bass, a snare hitting and sweeping time. In Bocchino's work the effect is similar, except hazy filmy colors have been pushed across the vellum surface, rather than contained at the center, creating the continuity of a moaning musical line.

A scribbled, innocent effect, echoing swirls and magic in Cy Twombly's elemental white on black paintings, is richly evident in Bocchino's *Romance Series*, from around 2001. An example from that series, *Untitled*, 2001, has layers of color and interference on the surface, and is composed of oil and graphite on vellum paper. Multiple revelations appear in paint, and then in linear design over that painted surface. On the final graphite layer, Bocchino interferes again with painted gold ovals, each varying slightly in hue, from rose-gold to crimson-copper, to verdigris. Under strong graphite lines, revelations of gray blue appear, as if smeared, greasy whale skin lies buried beneath a sandy and creamy smooth surface.

Following this group of paintings, Bocchino began to further ply the vellum, testing opacity and transparency of color against the smooth support. Her drawings on vellum surmount the exploration of color, always in circular motions, but often wiry, starting with small movements, and growing to larger ones, then becoming tangled and compressed as the horizontal expression continues. A small work from 2006, *Untitled BL002*, captures some exquisite expressions of line, married to lively Mediterranean blue, glints of orange and yellow light playing at the distant horizon.

Untitled, 2001
Oil and graphite on vellum paper
19 x 29 in.

Untitled for Missing Mingus, 2000
Oil and graphite on vellum paper
19 x 29 in.

Recent paintings from the *White on White Series* include enamel paint and gold leaf, sheets of mirror joined to canvas, or fragments of mirror visible on the finished surface. *Yesterday* appears to be divided into thirds, yet it is an asymmetrical diptych of a mirror panel joined with canvas. One third of the resulting whole is painted onto a cement gray brown background, softly warm and dark at the same time. The remaining two-thirds are built up on layers of creamy white, exploring the values of white paint. There are strings of glossy white enamel paint poured and drizzled over each portion, creating lyrical, dancing lines. Two panels are joined by this act of drawing over their surfaces,

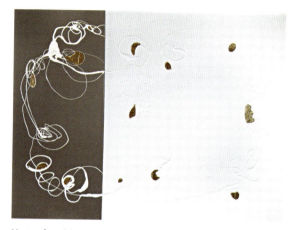

Yesterday, 2014
Enamel and gold leaf on mirror and canvas
42 x 52 in.

Pure Fall (White on White Series), 2013
Enamel with gold leaf on canvas
42 x 52 in.

linking them with threads of glossy white. Accents of gold leaf have been dotted into an embracing and containing place, as if an idea were caught in the tangle of moving line. These glints of light reflect from an otherwise matte surface.

Pure Fall, from 2013, also from the *White on White Series*, is interrupted with pockets of gold leaf against a white canvas, thickly ornamented with deliberate drips and swirls of creamy enamel paint. The effect is golden ash, falling from an unseen source above and to the right of the canvas. Bocchino connects the viewer to an unseen event, although she also conveys the simplicity of white line, against a plain canvas, with gold flakes falling through the viscous net of lines.

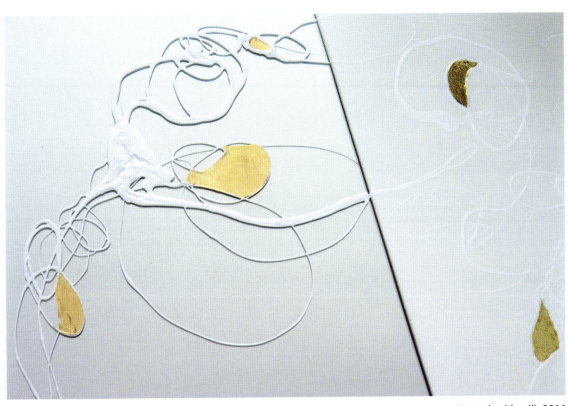

Yesterday (detail), 2014
Enamel and gold leaf on mirror and canvas

Tondo Mirror Installation, 2015
Enamel and gold leaf on mirrors and wood
9 tondos, 18 in. each

Rush Crush Rush, 2014
Monotype silkscreen, graphite with gold,
silver and copper leaf on birch wood
24 x 24 in.
Private Collection

Rush Crush, 2014
Monotype silkscreen, graphite with gold, silver and
copper leaf and diamond dust on birch wood
24 x 24 in.

Recent works include a series of square monotypes on birch wood. Constant innovation, fueled by an internal energy to expand her visual vocabulary, leads Bocchino to experiment with materials that often appear in precious objects, or decorative arts, rather then traditional paintings or prints. Bocchino's 2014 monotypes combine birch wood with silkscreen and delicate surface adhesions, merging unadorned wood with her linear expression in colored light on a surface.

Beginning with a square of simple, unvarnished birch wood, Bocchino silkscreens layers of ink and paint, before making final actions with rare and precious materials. One monotype, *Rush Crush Rush*, of 2014, features a combination of silkscreen technique and cumulative layers as a subtle foil to natural variation in wood. Delicate placement of gold, silver and copper leaf in the interior loops of white creates a luxurious polychrome experience, adorning the locus where wood grain, ink and paint intertwine. Another monotype from that series, *Rush Crush*, enhances the wooden object with an additional material: diamond dust. Reminding the viewer of Miró's pure color disks against linear doodles, glints of gold, silver, and copper add playful elements to the variegated grain of the wood.

Kiss (Romance Series), 2002
Enamel on canvas
30 x 40 in.

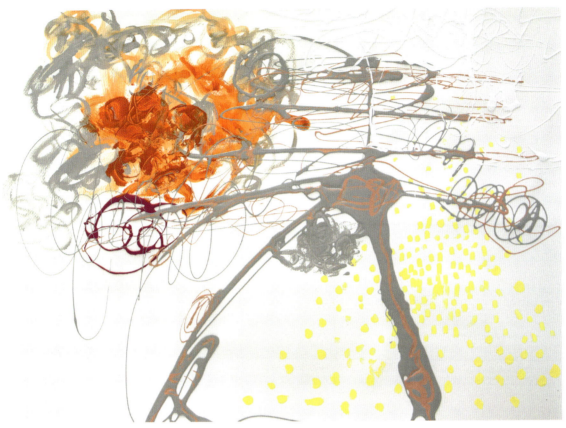

Untitled Orange/Gray, 2015
Enamel on rag paper
22 x 30 in.

Kiss, from the *Romance Series*, is a tangle of luscious white drips and strokes of enamel paint over a blue grey and magenta central effusion. Lines scattered and concentrated as layers accumulate, make this one of the more intriguing and energetic compositions, where small dots of orange explode outward from the heart of the painting. An allusion to Pollock is complicated by the very smooth quality of the paint, drips obviously poured and worked in great circling gestures, thick yet soft, like pulled taffy, in sweetly gooey hues.

Bocchino's most recent paintings, like *Untitled Orange/Gray* of 2015 in enamel on rag paper, are drizzled or layered accumulations of color, thickly applied to the delicate surface, with a luscious substance and vibrancy. In *Untitled Orange/Gray*, an orange red ball is placed above the middle, and the composition is dazzled with small linear forms at the periphery. The gray form at the heart, electrified with a pink flesh-toned line, appears to be composed of horizontal bars, swizzles of wiry designs, like mitts on multiple arms. Constant energy is present in works on paper or vellum and reflect an ongoing dialogue with the activated surface. Dots of yellow, speckled over creamy white, add to the movement of the gray figure at the center in *Untitled Orange/Gray*.

A new series of paintings emerging from Bocchino's studio provides the most seductive paint surfaces to date. *Over It*, from 2015, created in strong and rich colors of enamel, shows Bocchino drawing with the poured paint, affixing circular disks of mirror to the canvas, and then covering them with enamel tracings, or gestures of poured paint in lime green, flesh tones, and red against a base structure of dark blue. A black and blue structure occupies the first layer, and then a thickened and worried surface is filled with contrasting peach, pink and red, slipping over small intrusions of mirror, holding them to the surface with looping threads of color. Dots of white and silvered mirror pick up glints of light adding reflections to the surface.

Many of Bocchino's muses–Klee, Miró and Kline–worked with abstraction inspired by music, following the internal direction of a thought altered in the presence of sound. Each developed a particular response to sound and memory. Bocchino does this by painting in series, building on a certain theme, or mode of expression, like the recent *White on White Series*, or energetic, *Romance Series*. Yet some of her most lyrical compositions, like *Pure Fall*, of 2013, offer fresh interpretation of her own internal language. This painting in enamel with gold leaf, one of the *White on White Series*, features a surface built up in layers of white, varying the tones and depths of paint, leaving curls thickly applied to the surface with sweeping gestures. Accents of gold leaf pick out occasional ellipses or crescents formed by the intersection of lines that have their own direction. Not immediately discernable, enamel lines connect fragments of gold, subtly distributed over white surface below. Among Bocchino's different series, and the variety of her techniques, realms of physical experience are caught and held within her gestures.

Leaving the studio one afternoon, sun glinted from the snow outside Bocchino's window, and the clear inspiration for the dabs of gold leaf and radiant yellows of her palette became clear, and simple. Strains of music began as the door closed, and Bocchino returned to her work, interpreting sounds, interpreting gestures, and recording the bright energy of her spirit in paint.

Over It, 2015
Enamel and mirrors on canvas
42 x 32 in.

PUBLICATIONS
1986 to 2003

"The qualities of light and color in these paintings vibrate with an energy that seems Keplerian in inspiration. The merging of figure and ground through the use of short, painterly brushstrokes that delineate while obscuring form creates a synthesis that is enhanced by the subject matter: musical instruments".

Janet Gillespie
108 REVIEW, New York, NY
October 1986

Two Drums, 1986
Oil on canvas
46 x 46 in.
Private Collection

"In Serena Bocchino's paintings, musical instruments, such as bells, cellos and drums, hover behind a pictorial film like mementos of a paradise lost."

Michael Brenson
The New York Times
January 9, 1988

9 Bells, 1986
Oil on canvas
72 x 72 in.
Private Collection

Cracked House Looking Up, 1998
Oil on canvas
72 x 72 in.
Private Collection

"Their inspirations have been as diverse as the Italian Renaissance (Greene), French Impressionism (Bocchino) and Japanese Modernism (Voulkos), yet their individual traditions converge in 1950's American Abstract Expressionism. Bocchino's eight paintings at Penine Hart Gallery, all executed this year, harken back to a range of 19th and 20th century European and American Sources. But Bocchino cites Gottlieb, Rothko and Kline as her primary mentors. It may be old-fashioned, she told me, 'but I believe that the intellect, skill and spirit of an artist can be conveyed through a visual vocabulary.' Placing spiritual values over property values, Bocchino, still in her twenties, is in some sense an inheritor of the legacy of (70 year old) Greene and (64 year old) Voulkos."

Arlene Raven
"Family Values", *The Village Voice*, New York, NY
November 8, 1988

A Time to Weep, 1986
Oil on canvas
52 x 62 in.

"Rothenberg's choice Serena Bocchino was represented by a lucscious painting called 'Conga' seeing paint handled tastefully, intelligently and sensually is a pleasure. Sometimes I get the impression that many paintings don't allow themselves sensual and beautiful paintings out of mondernist guilt, a subconscious disease running rampant in the postmondernist community."

Andy Sichel Hindsites
Downtown Magazine, New York, NY
April 2, 1986

Reach Boat on Stilts, 1989
Oil on canvas
28 x 20 in.
Private Collection

"Most of Bocchino's pictures are distinguished in a formal sense by their elegant placement of compositional elements. However her pictures' most enticing lures are their auras of mystery, occasioned by the visionary character of her subjects and the loose, hallucinogenic approach to portraying them."

Roger Green
The Times-Picayune, St. Louis, MO
February 22, 1991

When/Now, 2002
Enamel and oil on canvas
32 x 50 in.

Untitled for Missing Mingus, 2000
Oil and graphite on vellum paper
19 x 29 in.

"Her light, gestural touch is a signature effect as are her muted blue-grays and melon colors, occasionally punctuated by bursts of orange or crimson; drawings done in oils on vellum have an even more atmospheric effect. Bocchino's work brings the 20th century's interest in the personal meaning of the brushstroke into the 21st."

Dan Bischoff
Star Ledger, Newark, NJ
January 2, 2000

"Serena Bocchino allows drizzled paint to weave linear motifs in her lively canvases. Lines accented with brilliant colors have a playful character. In 'Zooms and Booms', for example, the zigzag rhythm plays off against clouds of soft yellow, while in 'Right Away', loops and coils of color are sometimes buried under broad strokes of tan, only to re-emerge assertively."

Helen A. Harrison
The New York Times
November 23, 2003

Zooms and Booms, 2003
Enamel and oil on canvas
52 x 72 in.

Complete, 2002
Enamel and oil on canvas
52 x 72 in.

"Most fundamentally, the theme of the Morris exhibition is dance or I suppose we should say jazz, whose improvisational rhythms have inspired each painting. The act of painting them is very much like a four limbed dance, with the added appeal of ribbons of liquid color floating through the empty air—Bocchino gracefully lays down the paint with ecstatic abandon, punctuated occasionally by knuckled concentration."

Dan Bischoff
The Star Ledger, Newark, NJ
July 4, 2003

SEEING: EAST MEETS WEST

Lily Zhang

Three years ago, I came from China seeking a connection between the art of Asia and the art of the West. Shortly after arriving in New York, I was introduced to the work of Serena Bocchino. At first, I was not sure about her large paintings of poured enamel paint. The work was impressive; however, I did not fully understand the relationship of the graphite to the paint, nor was I certain about what she was trying to say through or with her paintings. Her pieces are very diverse from series to series and from one painting to the next, but they are also closely linked. What I could feel is her free spirit surging in the swirling enamel; her style reminds me of Chinese calligraphy.

The decorative side of her work has some similarity with Chinese lacquer painting and also possesses the luxurious feeling of an antique decorative vase. As I came to know Bocchino's new work, I began to understand her process and intellectual motivation. I came to know the spiritual dynamic that she passionately pours out onto the canvas. These two characteristics of her work are historically ever present in Chinese work. Although Bocchino does not "know" the Chinese contemporary market, the language she employs in her creations has an impact similar to the art I have seen in Beijing. Being part of the development of the 798 Art District in Beijing, China, I am familiar with many emerging and mid-career artists like Serena Bocchino. She shares with them a mastery of technique and ideology that seems to be universal for accomplished artists. Her drive and art-making methodology is uniquely American; however, her poetry and passion are similar to qualities found in Chinese art.

As the editor of this book project, I was able to journey with Serena Bocchino to her beginnings as an artist. Her path moves from influences from her artist mother, to art lessons as a teen to college and graduate school training to her professional career beginning in the East Village in New York. Noting her experiences as a young artist and seeing the many periods of art-making that she has participated in, and viewing the parallels of her life in relation to her professional career, Bocchino's commitment to her practice is clear.

Chinese calligraphy is regarded as the most abstract and sublime form of art: "The way characters are written is a portrait of the writer." Calligraphy reflects a person's emotions, moral integrity, character, education level, accomplishments, personal cultivation, and even their approach to life.

Knowing my calligraphic tradition allows me to see the relationship of Bocchino's work to Chinese calligraphy because she creates her work as a reflection of who she is. As she pours paint and draws with graphite or charcoal, she skillfully embraces each mark with her whole being.

It has been revitalizing to work on this project because it has given me a clear picture of the connection between Asia and the West. By recognizing Bochhino's life work as it has developed over the years, I have gained a new insight into a whole generation of American artists working in New York. It has been a privilege to work with Jonathan Goodman and Lisa Banner, whose knowledge and expertise has helped me to see the career of an artist committed to creating a language of her own and the maturation of her professional career spanning over 25 years.

PAINTINGS AND INSTALLATIONS

2015 to 1987

Sometimes Magenta, 2011
Enamel on canvas
30 x 40 in.

Field of Blue, 2011
Enamel on canvas
30 x 40 in.

Orange Crossing Blue, 2015
Enamel on canvas
32 x 42 in.

Early Yellow, 2015
Enamel on canvas
44 x 60 in.

Amazing Alternative, 2015
Enamel on canvas
40 x 30 in.

Smoke and Orange, 2015
Enamel on canvas
42 x 32 in.

Soar, 2015
Enamel and mirrors on canvas
28 x 34 in.

Previous page:
Synchronous Hug, 2015
Enamel and mirrors on canvas
60 x 80 in.

Star Balance Moves, 2015
Enamel and mirrors on canvas
42 x 52 in.
Private Collection

Bocchino working on *iPOP Series*, 2008

Synchronicity, 2009
Enamel on canvas
80 x 60 in.
Private Collection

Zoe Life, 2004
Enamel on canvas
52 x 72 in.
Private Collection

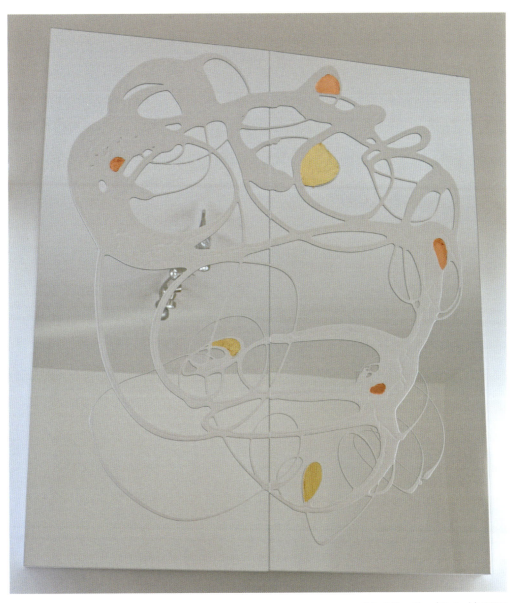

Meet Together (Diptych), 2015
Enamel, gold and copper leaf on mirrors
42 x 36 in.

Artist drawing with graphite on canvas, 2013

Romeo (Fever Series), 2012
Enamel, graphite and gold leaf on canvas
32 x 42 in.

Dancing Duets in Red and White, 2011
Enamel and graphite on canvas
26 x 24 in.

Painting in progress for film documentary, 2013
Hoboken Studio

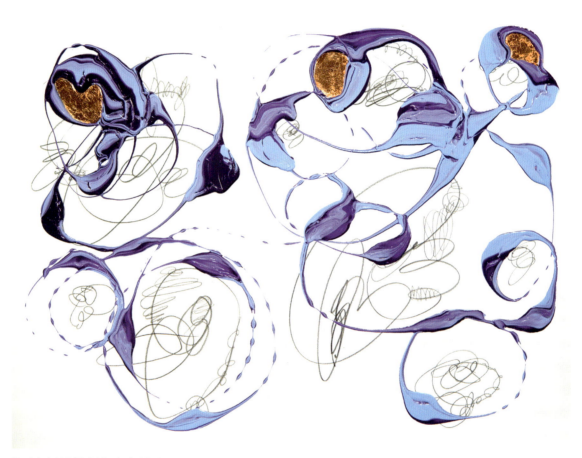

Untitled 005 (Twirl Series), 2014
Enamel and copper leaf on rag paper
22 x 30 in.

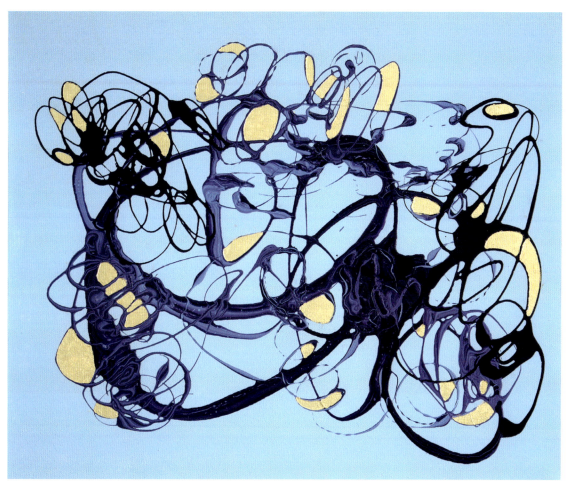

At the Sound of Light, 2014
Enamel and gold leaf on canvas
30 x 36 in.

iPOP Installation, 2009
Tria Gallery
New York, NY

iPOP Installation, 2011
Center for Contemporary Art
Bedminster, NJ

Wild (iPOP Series), 2008
Enamel on canvas
49 x 62 in.

Outside Orange with figurines (iPOP Series), 2009
Tria Gallery
New York, NY
Private Collection

Breathe Mural Installation, 2004
108 x 192 in.
Jersey City Medical Center, NJ

Rhythm Rain TCR Box, 2010
86 x 60 x 56 in.
Public Installation

Artist in studio, 2008

Orange Burst, 2009
Enamel on canvas
46 x 49 in.
Private Collection

Rhythm Rain (iPOP Series), 2009; Enamel on canvas; 30 x 40 in. (left)
Garden Blue (iPOP Series), 2008; Enamel on acrylic sheet; 30 x 36 in. (right)

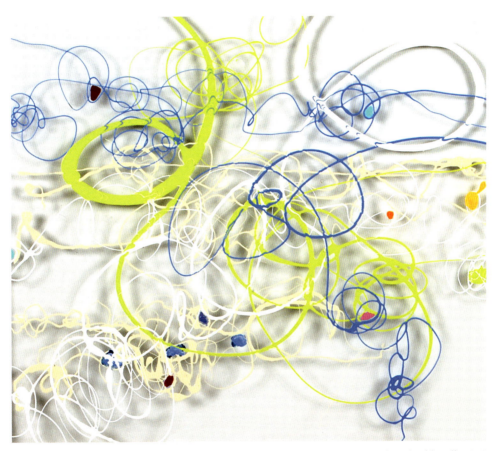

Garden Blue (detail), 2008
Enamel on acrylic sheet

Casting Out (Catch Series), 2007
Enamel and oil on canvas
52 x 54 in.
Private Collection

Blue Fountains and Mountains (Catch Series), 2007
Enamel and oil on canvas
52 x 65 in.

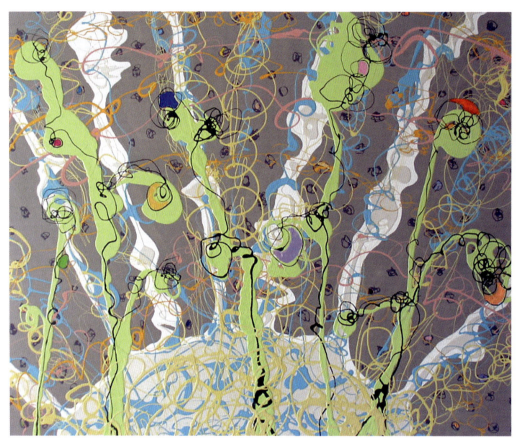

Good Morning, 2001
Enamel and oil on canvas
42 x 52 in.

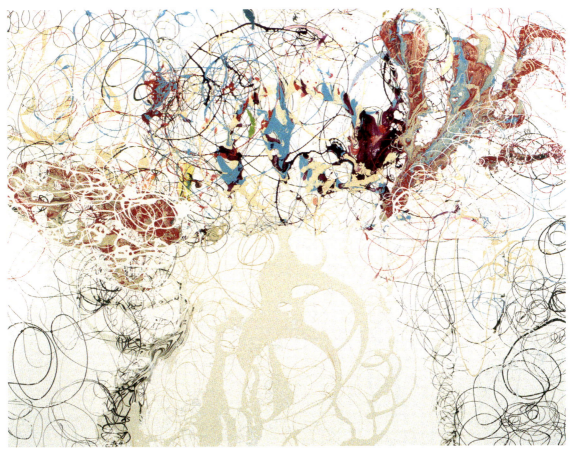

Interruption, 2003
Enamel on canvas
52 x 65 in.
Private Collection

Moving Mountains, 2000
Enamel and oil on canvas
52 x 72 in.
Private Collection

All the Time, 1999
Enamel and oil on canvas
28 x 34 in.
Private Collection

Red Sea, 1993
Oil and mixed media on canvas
40 x 60 in.
Private Collection

Boxing God, 1993
Oil and mixed media on canvas
60 x 80 in.
Private Collection

Deuces, 1998
Oil and mixed media on canvas
52 x 56 in.
Private Collection

Cool Baker Bridge, 1998
Oil and mixed media on canvas
52 x 56 in.
Private Collection

Strings, 1993
Oil and mixed media on canvas
72 x 72 in.
Private Collection

Cage Silence, 1997
Oil and mixed media on canvas
56 x 52 in.
Private Collection

Untitled, 1991
Graphite and oil on vellum
11 x 14 in.

Wall Painting Installation (Water Island Series), 1991
Oil, graphite, charcoal and collage on sheetrock
84 x 156 in.

Three Yellow Bursts, 1989
Oil on canvas
40 x 30 in.

SaxSex, 1987
Oil on canvas
48 x 46 in.
Private Collection

A Time to Weep, 1986
Oil on canvas
52 x 65 in.

Boat at the Top, 1989
Oil on canvas
72 x 70 in.
Private Collection

DRAWINGS AND PRINTS
2015 to 1987

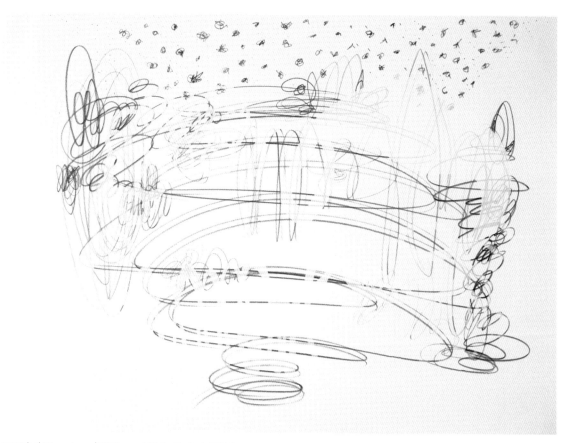

Untitled Monotype (White on White Series), 2014
Monotype silkscreen and graphite on rag paper
22 x 30 in.

Rush Crush Rush, 2014
Monotype silkscreen, graphite with gold, silver
and copper leaf on birch wood
24 x 24 in.
Private Collection

Untitled 0016 (White on White Series), 2014
Enamel and gold leaf on rag paper
22 x 30 in.

Simpatico, 2003
Lithography, silkscreen, pochoir and embossing
22 x 30 in.

Untitled Green Squeegee Drawing, 1993
Oil paint and graphite on rag paper
22 x 30 in.

Untitled, 1998
Oil and graphite on vellum
19 x 29 in.

Untitled Monotype (White on White Series), 2014
Monotype silkscreen and graphite on rag paper
22 x 30 in.

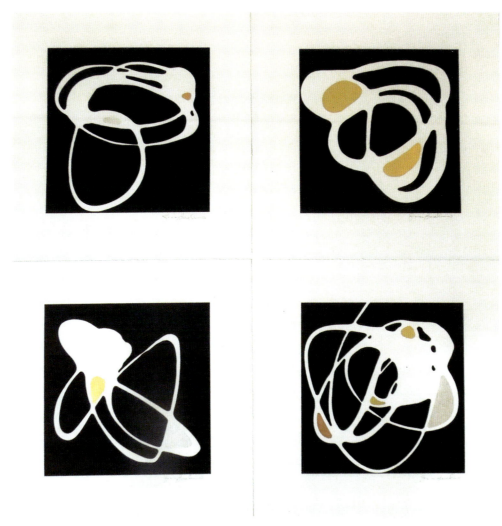

Quartet, 2014
Lithography and silver, gold and copper leaf
Set of 4, 18 x 18 in. each

Charcoal Interior, 1987
Charcoal and graphite on rag paper
22 x 29 in.

Charcoal Lyrical, 1988
Charcoal and graphite on rag paper
22 x 29 in.

Conga, 1988
Charcoal and graphite on rag paper
22 x 29 in.

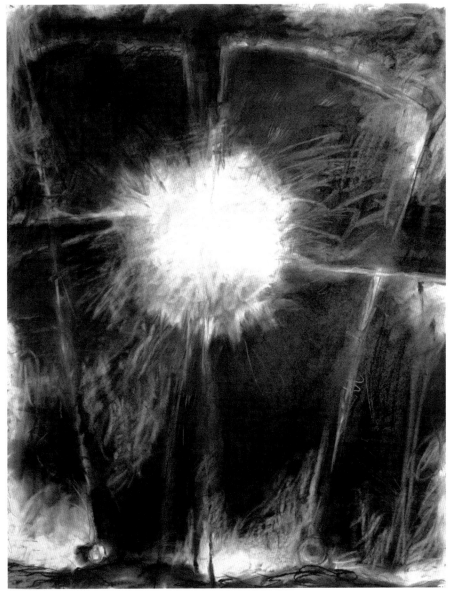

Burst, 1989
Charcoal and graphite on rag paper
22 x 29 in.

SERENA BOCCHINO

EDUCATION
1985   Master of Arts, New York University, NYC
1982   Bachelor of Arts, Honors College, Fairleigh Dickinson University, Teaneck, NJ
           Thesis: *A Study of Painting Techniques*
1982   Art Research Sabbatical: Moscow, Leningrad, Suzdal, Vladimir
1980   Wroxton College, Oxfordshire, England

AWARDS
2013   Excellence in the Arts Award, New Jersey
2002   Fellowship, New Jersey State Council on the Arts
           Residency, The Brodsky Center, Rutgers University
1994   Trenton City Museum Award given by Lois Dodd
           AIE, New Jersey State Council on the Arts
1990   The Basil H. Alkazzi Award, USA
           Artists Space/Artists Grant, NYC
1989   Pollock-Krasner Grant, NYC
           Nomination, Louis Comfort Tiffany Award, NYC
           Art Matters Grant, NYC
1988   Artists Space/Artists Grant, NYC
1987   Residency Program, PS1 Studio Program, NYC
           Finalist, Prix de Rome
           Finalist, Award in the Visual Arts, NYC
1985   Fellowship, New Jersey State Council on the Arts
1980   Wroxton College Award, Oxfordshire, England

PUBLIC ART COMMISSIONS
2013   PWR, Washington D.C.
2011   Moelis, New York, NY
2010   Gallery 24/7 Public Project TCR Boxes, NJ
2005-08   Falconhead, Park Avenue, New York, NY
2008   Riverfront, One Main Street, Cambridge, MA
2005   Hines Building, New York, NY
2004   The Jersey City Medical Center, Jersey City, NJ
2003-04   Pfizer Inc, Morris Plains, NJ and New York, NY

SOLO EXHIBITIONS
2015   ART MORA, New York, NY
2014   ARTHAUS, San Francisco, CA
2013   Contemporary Art and Editions, NJ
2012   Simon Gallery Morristown, NJ
2011   Center for Contemporary Art, NJ
2010   Simon Gallery, Morristown, NJ
2009   Tria Gallery, New York, NY
2008   Art Assets, Cambridge, MA
2007   Tria Gallery, New York, NY
           ArtHaus, San Francisco, NY
2005   The Morris Museum, Morristown, NJ
2004   Pfizer Inc, New York, NY
2003   Pfizer Inc, Morris Plains, NJ
           Exhibit A, New York, NY
           The Morris Museum, Morristown, NJ
           Delaware Center for Contemporary Arts, Wilmington, DE
2000   Jeffrey Coploff Fine Art, New York, NY
           Exhibit A, New York, NY
1999   Jeffrey Coploff Fine Art, New York, NY
           Galerie du Tableau, Marseille, France
           ArtHaus, San Francisco, CA
1998   Ben Shahn Gallery, WPU, Wayne, NJ
           Chubb Corporation, Warren, NJ
1997   Jeffrey Coploff Fine Art, New York, NY
1995-96   Special Projects, New York, NY
           Bergen Museum of Art and Science, NJ
           Trenton City Museum, NJ
           Princeton University, Princeton, NJ
1994   Rabbet Gallery, New Brunswick, NJ
1992   Johnson & Johnson, Skillman, NJ
1991   Sylvia Schmidt Gallery, New Orleans, LA
1990   Penine Hart Gallery, New York, NY
           Phyllis Rothman Gallery, FDU, NJ
           Studio Bocchi, Rome, Italy
1989   Elliot Smith Gallery, St. Louis, MO
1988   Penine Hart Gallery, New York, NY
1987   The Maples Gallery, FDU Teaneck, NJ
1986   Jus de Pomme Gallery, New York, NY
1985   80 Washington Square Galleries, NY

FILM DOCUMENTARIES ABOUT THE ARTIST

FEVER
Directed by Greg Smith
Produced by Greg Smith/Down the Line Productions
Edited by Jason Schuler/Awakened Films
Music by Peggy Lee

A Dream of Blue*
Directed by Monica Sharf and Greg Smith
Produced by Greg Smith, Down the Line Productions
Edited by David Leonard
Music by Pat Metheny
*Best Inspirational Short Award, NYIIFVF

Observer Highway Revisited
Directed and Produced by Monica Sharf, Inversion Films
Cinematography by Thomas Moore
Edited by Rachel DeSario/Version 2 Editing, New York, NY
Music by Clifford Brown and Max Roach

Observer Highway: Portrait of Serena Bocchino
Directed by Yvette Pineyro and Pavel Salek
Produced and Edited by Yvette Pineyro
    Wildchild Editorial, New York
Music by Peter Gabriel

iPOP
Catavideo for iPOP Exhibition, Tria Gallery New York, NY
Directed and Produced by Greg Smith/Down the Line
    Productions and Tria Gallery, New York, NY,
Photography, Cinematography, Effects and Editing by
    Jason Schuler/ Awakened Films
Music by Pat Metheny

What is iPop
Directed by Mark DePasquale Films
Produced by The Center for Contemporary Art,
    Bedminster, NJ

Rhythms
Directed and Produced by Yvette Pineyro and Pavel Salek
Edited by Yvette Pineyro at Wildchild Editorial
    Studios. Inc. New York, NY

BOOKS AND PUBLISHED ARTICLES
Who Am I? The Story of the Artist, 2011
What Am I? The Story of an Abstract Painting, 2011
*M/E/A/N/I/N/G A Journal of Contemporary Art
    Issues, #20*, 1995
*M/E/A/N/I/N/G A Journal of Contemporary Art
    Issues, #16*, 1994

PUBLIC COLLECTIONS
Art in Embassies Program, Lima, Peru
Bergen Museum, Paramus, NJ
Duff & Phelps, Chicago, IL
Forrester Morrison, New York, NY
Fidelity Investments Jersey City, NJ
Hunterdon Art Museum, Clinton, NJ
IBJ Schroder Bank & Trust, New York, NY
Islip Art Museum, East Islip, NY
Janssen Pharmaceuticals, Warrenville, NJ
Jersey City Museum, Jersey City, NJ
Johnson & Johnson, New Brunswick, NJ
KPG Peat Marwick, Minneapolis, MN
McKinsey & Co. Incorporated, New York, NY
Moelis International, New York, NY
Montclair Art Museum, Montclair, NJ
Morris Museum, Morristown, NJ
Newark Museum, Newark, NJ
NJ State Council on the Arts, Trenton, NJ
Nordstrom, Seattle, WA
Noyes Museum, Oceanville, NJ
Pensare, Palo Alto, CA
Pfizer Inc, New York, NY
Plaid Brothers, San Francisco, CA
PriceWaterhouse and Coopers, New York, NY
Redback Networks Inc., Sunnyvale, CA
Saks Fifth Avenue, New York, NY
Springfield Museum of Art, Springfield, OH
The Paterson Art Museum, Paterson, NJ
The Prudential, Newark, NJ
The Brodsky Center, New Brunswick, NJ
Trenton City Museum, Trenton, NJ
Trenton State Museum, Trenton, NJ
Warburg Pincus Ventures Inc., New York, NY
Westcliff Realities, Montreal, Quebec, Canada
Wildchild Inc., New York, NY
Zimmerli Art Museum, New Brunswick, NJ